The Tales of Hoffmann

Jules Barbier

Translated by Charles Alfred Byrne

NEW VERSION
OF
Les Contes d'Hoffmann
(THE TALES OF HOFFMAN)
OPERA IN FOUR ACTS

———————

With an original and novel first Act and other important changes

———————

Book by JULES BARBIER

MUSIC BY

J. OFFENBACH

New English version by CHARLES ALFRED BYRNE

———————

ENGLISH VERSION, 1907

DRAMATIS PERSONÆ.

HOFFMANN

COUNSELOR LINDORF

COPPELIUS

DAPERTUTTO

DOCTOR MIRACLE

SPALANZANI

CRESPEL

ANDRES

COCHENILLE

FRANTZ

LUTHER

NATHANAEL

HERMANN

STELLA

GIULIETTA

OLYMPIA

ANTONIA

NICKLAUSSE

THE MUSE

A GHOST

ARGUMENT

ACT I.

In the first act, which is really a prologue, Hoffmann, a young poet, enters the tavern of Luther to meet his companions, and drinks to drown his sorrows. They think he is in love, but he answers, all that is past, and tells the story of his three loves.

ACT II. OLYMPIA.

A physician's drawing room. Spalanzani has invited a large company to witness the accomplishments of his daughter, Olympia. She sings to general applause, and Hoffmann falls desperately in love with her. As the guests go to supper, Hoffmann tells her of his passion and thinks he finds a responsive echo in her. There is dancing, and she waltzes him off his feet. A Dr. Coppelius comes in to say he has been swindled by Spalanzani. He slips into Olympia's room, from which a noise of breaking is heard. Coppelius, out of revenge, has smashed Olympia. She was only an automaton. Hoffmann is astonished.

ACT III. GIULIETTA.

At Venice, in the house of Giulietta, beloved of Schlemil, who takes the arrival of Hoffmann very ungraciously. Hoffmann cares nothing for Giulietta, but she is bribed by Dapertutto to make Hoffmann love her, and she succeeds by making him believe, that he is her ideal. But as a proof of his love she wants Hoffmann to get the key of her room away from Schlemil. Hoffmann demands the key; Schlemil tells him to come and take it, and they fight. Schlemil is killed. Hoffmann takes the key and rushes to Giulietta's room, and finding nobody, comes back, only to see her riding off in her gondola, laughing at him, and with her arms around another man's neck. Hoffmann is disgusted.

ACT IV. ANTONIA.

Antonia has been told by her father, Crespel, to sing no more. When Hoffmann, who has long loved her, comes, he wonders why, but he soon learns by overhearing a conversation between Crespel and an evil person called Doctor Miracle that Antonia is afflicted with consumption. He then begs her also not to sing, and she promises him. When Hoffmann goes, Miracle comes in and tells her it is all nonsense, to sing as much as she likes; but she will not break her promise to Hoffmann. Miracle then causes the ghost of Antonia's mother to appear, and to her prayers the girl yields. Miracle urges her on and on, until she is utterly exhausted. She falls dying, and her father receives her last breath. Hoffmann is heartbroken.

EPILOGUE.

A return to the scene of the first act. Hoffmann has told his stories. His companions leave him. The Muse appears and tells him that she is the only mistress to follow, the only one who will remain true to him. His spirit flickers a moment with gratitude. Then his head sinks on the table, and he sleeps.

ACT I.

(The Tavern of Martin Luther. The interior of a German inn. Tables and benches.)

CHORUS of Students.

Drig, drig, drig, master Luther,
   Spark of hades,
Drig, drig, drig, for us more beer,
   For us thy wine,
   Until morning,
   Fill my glass,
   Until morning,
Fill our pewter Mugs!

NATHANAEL.

Luther is a brave man,
   Tire, lan, laire,
T'is to-morrow that we brain him,
   Tire, lan, la!

CHORUS.

   Tire, lon, la!

LUTHER (going from table to table).

  Here, gentlemen, here.

HERMANN.

His cellar is a goodly spot,
   Tire lon, laire,
'Tis tomorrow we devast it,
   Tire lon la!

CHORUS.

Tire lon la!

(Knocking of glasses.)

LUTHER.

Here, gentlemen, here.

WILHELM.

His wife is a daughter of Eve,
    Tire lan laire,
'Tis to-morrow we abduct her,
    Tire lon la.

CHORUS.

Tire lon la!

LUTHER.

Here, gentlemen, here.

CHORUS.

Drig, drig, drig, master Luther,
    etc., etc.

(The students sit drinking and smoking.)

NATHANAEL.

And Luther, my goodly vat,
What have you done with our Hoffman.

HERMANN.

T'is your wine poisoned him,
You've killed him faith of Herrmann,
Give us back Hoffmann.

ALL.

Give us Hoffmann.

LINDORF (aside).

To the devil, Hoffmann.

NATHANAEL.

Let them bring him to us
Or your last day has dawned.

LUTHER.

Gentlemen, he comes.

(He opens the door, and Nicklausse is with him.)

ALL.

Hurrah, 'tis he.

LINDORF (aside).

Let's watch him.

HOFFMANN (entering with sombre voice).

Good day, friends.

NICKLAUSSE.

 Good-day.

HOFFMANN.

A chair, a glass,
A pipe...

NICKLAUSSE (mocking).

Pardon, my lord, without displeasing,
I drink, smoke and sit like you... place for two.

CHORUS.

 He's right... place for both of them.

(Hoffmann and Nicklausse sit down, Hoffmann has head in his hands.)

NICKLAUSSE (humming).

 Notte a giorno mal dormire...

HOFFMANN (brusquely).

 Shut up, in devil's name.

NICKLAUSSE (quietly).

 Yes, master.

HERMANN (to Hoffmann).

 Oh, oh, whence comes this ill temper?

NATHANAEL (to Hoffmann).

It's as if one did not know you.

HERMANN.

On what thorn have you trod?

HOFFMANN.

Alas, on a dead herb
With the iced breath of the north.

NICKLAUSSE.

And there by this door,
On a drunkard who sleeps.

HOFFMANN.

'Tis true... that rascal, by Jove, I envy him.
A drink. Like him, let's sleep in the gutter.

HERMANN.

Without pillow.

HOFFMANN.

The flags.

NATHANAEL.

Without curtains.

HOFFMANN.

 The sky.

NATHANAEL.

 The rain.

HERMANN.

 Have you a nightmare, Hoffmann?

HOFFMANN.

No, but to-night,
A while since, at the play...

ALL.

 Well?

HOFFMANN.

 I thought to see again...
The deuce... why reopen old wounds?
Life is short. Enjoy it while we can.
We must drink, sing, laugh, as we may,
Left to weep to-morrow!

NATHANAEL.

Then sing the first without asking,
We'll do chorus.

HOFFMANN.

Agreed!

NATHANAEL.

Something gay.

HERMANN.

The song of the Rat!

NATHANAEL.

No, for me, I'm tired of it.
What we want is the legend
Of Klein-Zach...

ALL.

'Tis the legand of Klein-Zach.

HOFFMANN.

Here goes for Klein-Zach!...
Once at the court of Eysenach
A little dwarf called Klein-Zach,
Was covered o'er with a colbac,
And his legs they went clic, clac!
   Clic, clac.
There's Klein-Zach.

CHORUS.

Crick, crack,
There's Klein-Zach.

HOFFMANN.

He had a hump in place of stomach,
His webbed feet seemed to burst a sack,
His nose was with tobacco black.
And his head it went crick crack,
  Crick, crack.
There's Klein-Zach.

CHORUS.

  Crick, crack,
There's Klein-Zach.

HOFFMANN.

As for the features on his face.

(He becomes absorbed.)

CHORUS.

  As for the features on his face.

HOFFMANN (very slowly).

  As for the features...

(He rises.)

Oh, her face was charming... I see it,
Fine as the day, running after her,
I, like a fool, left the house paternal,
And fled there'on to woods and vales
Her hair, in sombre rolls,
On her neck threw warm shades,
Her eyes of enveloping azure,
Cast about glances fresh and pure.
And as our car without shock or tremor

Carried our loves and hearts, her vibrant voice and sweet,
To the heav'ns that listened, threw the conq'ring cry,
And the eternal echo resounded in my heart.

NATHANAEL.

Oh strangest brain!
Who are you painting! Klein-Zach?

HOFFMANN.

 I speak of her...

NATHANAEL.

 Who?

HOFFMANN.

Nobody... nothing, my spirit is dullish.
Nothing. Klein-Zach is better, malformed as he is!

CHORUS.

 Flick, flack,
 There's Klein-Zach.

HOFFMANN (throwing away his glass).

Peuh!... this beer is detestable,
Let's light up the punch and drink;
And may the light-headed
Roll under the table.

CHORUS.

And may the light headed
Roll under the table.

CHORUS.

(The lights go out, Luther fires an immense punch bowl.)

Luther is a brave man,
   Tire la laire,
   Tire lan la.
'Tis to-morrow that we poison him,
   Tire lan laire,
   Tire lan la.
His cellar is a goodly spot,
   Tire lan laire.
'Tis to-morrow we will make it hot,
   Tire lan laire,
   Tire lan la.

NICKLAUSSE.

Very good, indeed. At least we are pruned
With reason and practical sense!
Away with languorous hearts.

NATHANAEL.

Let's wager that Hoffmann's in love.

HOFFMANN.

 What then?

NATHANAEL.

You need not blush, I imagine

Our friend Wilhelm who's there,
Burns for Leonor and finds her divine.
Hermann loves Gretchen and I am near ruined
For the Fausta.

HOFFMANN (to Wilhelm).

  Yes, Leonor, thy virtuose.

(To Hermann.)

Yes, Gretchen, thy doll inert, of icy heart.

(to Nathanael.)

And thy Fausta, poor insensate,
The courtezan with front of brass.

NATHANAEL.

  Morose spirit,
Many thanks for Fausta, Gretchen and Leonore!...

HOFFMANN.

  Pish. They are all alike.

NATHANAEL.

Then your mistress is such a treasure
That you despise so much our own?

HOFFMANN.

My mistress, no, no, say rather three
Charming trio of enchantresses.
Who are dividing my days.
Would you like the story of my crazy loves?...

CHORUS.

 Yes, yes!

NICKLAUSSE.

 What are you saying of three mistresses?

HOFFMANN.

 Smoke!...
Before this dead pipe is relighted
You will have comprehended,
You who in this play where my heart was consumed
In good sense took the first prize!

(All the students go to their places.)

CHORUS.

Listen. It is nice to drink,
To the telling of a crazy tale,
While following the fragrant cloud,
That a pipe throws in the air.

HOFFMANN (sitting on corner of table).

 I begin.

CHORUS.

 Silence.

HOFFMANN.

 The name of the first was Olympia...

(The curtain falls as Hoffmann is speaking.)

ACT II.

(A physicians room, richly furnished.)

HOFFMAN (alone).

Come! Courage and confidence;
I become a well of science.
I must turn with the wind that blows,
To deserve the one I love.
I shall know how to find in myself
The stuff of a learned man.
She is there... if I dared.

(He softly lifts the portiere.)

'Tis she!
She sleeps... how beautiful!
Ah! together live... both in the same hope,
The same remembrance
Divide our happiness and our sorrow,
And share the future.
Let, let my flame
Pour in thee the light,
Let your soul but open
To the rays of Love.
Divine hearth! Sun whose ardor penetrates
And comes to kiss us.
Ineffable desire where one's whole being
Melts in a single kiss.
Let, let my flame,
  etc., etc.

(Nicklausse appears.)

NICKLAUSSE.

By Jove, I felt sure you'd be here.

HOFFMAN (letting portiere fall).

Chut.

NICKLAUSSE.

Why? 'tis there that breathes
The dove who's now your amorous care,
The beautiful Olympia? Go, my child, admire!

HOFFMAN.

Yes, I adore her!

NICKLAUSSE.

Want to know her better.

HOFFMAN.

The soul one loves is easy to know.

NICKLAUSSE.

What? by a look... through a window?

HOFFMAN.

A look is enough to embrace the heavens.

NICKLAUSSE.

What warmth!... At least she knows that you love her.

HOFFMAN.

No.

NICKLAUSSE.

Write her.

HOFFMAN.

I don't dare.

NICKLAUSSE.

Poor lamb! Speak to her.

HOFFMAN.

The dangers are the same.

NICKLAUSSE.

Then sing, to get out of the scrape.

HOFFMAN.

Monsieur Spalanzani doesn't like music.

NICKLAUSSE (laughing).

Yes, I know, all for physics!
A doll with china eyes
Played cleverly with a fan,
Nearby a little cock in brass;
Both sang in unison
In a marvelous way,

Danced, gossiped, seemed to live.

HOFFMAN.

  Beg your pardon. Why this song?

NICKLAUSSE.

The little cock shining and smart,
With a very knowing air,
Three times on himself turned;
By some ingenious wheels,
The doll in rolling its eyes
Sighed and said: "I love you."

CHORUS OF THE INVITED GUESTS.

No, no host, really,
Receives more richly
Through good taste his house shines;
Everything here matches.
No, no host really
Receives more richly.

SPALANZANI.

  You will be satisfied, gentlemen, in a moment.

(He makes sign to Cochenille to follow him and exits with him.)

NICKLAUSSE (to Hoffman).

  At last we shall more nearly see this marvel
Without equal!

HOFFMAN.

  Silence... she is here!

(Enter Spalanzani conducting Olympia.)

SPALANZANI.

Ladies and gentlemen,
I present to you
My daughter Olympia.

THE CHORUS.

  Charming.
She has beautiful eyes!
Her shape is very good!
See how well apparelled!
Nothing is wanting!
She does very well!

HOFFMAN.

  Ah, how adorable she is!

NICKLAUSSE.

  Charming, incomparable!

SPALANZANI (to Olympia).

  What a success is thine!

NICKLAUSSE (taking her all in).

  Really she does very well.

THE CHORUS.

She has beautiful eyes,
Her shape is very good,
See how well apparelled,
Nothing is really wanting;
She does very well.

SPALANZANI.

Ladies and gentlemen, proud of your applause,
And above all anxious
To conquer more,
My daughter obedient to your least caprice
Will, if you please...

NICKLAUSSE (aside).

  Pass to other exercises.

SPALANZANI.

Sing to a grand air, following with the voice,
    Rare talent
The clavichord, the guitar,
Or the harp, at your choice!

COCHENILLE (at the rear).

The harp!

BASS VOICE (in the wings).

The harp!

SPALANZANI.

Very good, Cochenille!
Go quickly and bring my daughter's harp!

(Cochenille exits).

HOFFMAN (aside).

I shall hear her... oh joy!

NICKLAUSSE (aside).

Oh, crazy passion!

SPALANZANI (to Olympia).

Master your emotion, my child!

OLYMPIA.

Yes.

COCHENILLE (bringing the harp).

There!

SPALANZANI (sitting beside Olympia).

Gentlemen, attention!

COCHENILLE.

Attention!

THE CHORUS.

Attention!

OLYMPIA (accompanied by Spalanzani).

The birds in the bushes.
In the heavens the orb of day,
All speaks to the young girl
Of love, of love!
  There!
The pretty song,
  There!
The song of Olympia,
  Ha!

THE CHORUS.

'Tis the song of Olympia!

OLYMPIA.

All that sings and resounds
Has its sighs in turn,
Moves its heart that trembles
  With love.
  There.
The little song,
  There, there,
  The song of Olympia,
    Ha!

CHORUS.

'Tis the song of Olympia.

HOFFMAN (to Nicklausse).

Ah, my friend, what an accent.

NICKLAUSSE.

What runs!

(Cochenille has taken the harp and all surround Olympia. A servant speaks to Spalanzani).

Come gentlemen! your arm to the ladies.
Supper awaits you!

THE CHORUS.

Supper! That's good...

SPALANZANI.

Unless you would prefer
To dance first.

THE CHORUS (with energy).

No! no! the supper... good thing...
After we'll dance.

SPALANZANI.

As you please...

HOFFMAN (approaching Olympia).

Might I dare...

SPALANZANI (interrupting).

She is a bit tired,
Wait for the ball.

(He touches Olympia's shoulder.)

OLYMPIA.

Yes.

SPALANZANI.

You see. Until then
Will you do me the favor
To keep company with my Olympia?

HOFFMAN.

Oh happiness!

SPALANZANI (aside, laughing).

We'll see what kind a story he'll give her.

NICKLAUSSE (to Spalanzani).

Won't she take supper?

SPALANZANI.

No.

NICKLAUSSE (aside).

Poetic soul!

(Spalanzani goes behind Olympia. Noise of a spring is heard. Nicklausse turns around.)

What did you say?

SPALANZANI.

Nothing, physics! ah, monsieur, physics!

(He conducts Olympia to a chair. Goes out with guests).

COCHENILLE.

The supper awaits you.

THE CHORUS.

Supper, supper, supper awaits us!
No, really, no host
Receives more richly!

(They go out.)

HOFFMAN.

They are at last gone. Ah, I breathe!
Alone, alone, the two of us (approaching Olympia);
I have so many things to say,
Oh my Olympia! Let me admire you!
With your charming looks let me intoxicate myself.

(He touches her shoulder).

OLYMPIA.

Yes.

HOFFMAN.

Is it not a dream born of fever?
I thought I heard a sigh escape your lips!

(He again touches her shoulder).

OLYMPIA.

 Yes.

HOFFMAN.

Sweet avowal, pledge of our love,
You are mine, our hearts are united forever!
Ah! understand you, tell me, this eternal joy
Of silent hearts.
Living, with but one soul and with same stroke of wing,
Rush up to heaven!
Let, let, my flame
Show you the light of day!
Let your soul open
To the rays of love.

(He presses Olympia's hand. She rises and walks up and down, then exits.)

You escape me?... What have I done.
  You do not answer?...
Speak! Have I wounded you? Ah!
  I'll follow your steps!

(As Hoffmann is about to rush out Nicklausse appears.)

NICKLAUSSE.

Here, by Jove, moderate your zeal!
Do you want us to drink without you?...

HOFFMAN (half crazy).

Nicklausse, I am beloved by her.
Loved! By all the gods.

NICKLAUSSE.

By my faith
If you knew what they are saying of your beauty!

HOFFMAN.

What can they say? What?

NICKLAUSSE.

That she is dead.

HOFFMAN.

Great Heavens!

NICKLAUSSE.

Or is not of this life.

HOFFMAN (exalted).

Nicklausse! I am beloved by her!
Loved! By all the gods.

COPPÉLIUS (entering, furious).

Thief! brigand! what a tumble!
Elias is bankrupt!
But I shall find the opportunity

To revenge myself... Robbed!... Me!
  I'll kill somebody.

(Coppelius slips into Olympia's room.)

(Everybody enters.)

SPALANZANI.

  Here come the waltzers.

COCHENILLE.

  Here comes the round dance.

HOFFMAN.

  'Tis the waltz that calls us.

SPALANZANI (to Olympia).

  Take the hand of the gentleman, my child.

(Touching her shoulder.)

  Come.

OLYMPIA.

  Yes.

(Hoffman takes Olympia and they waltz. They disappear on left.)

CHORUS.

  She dances!
  In cadence.

'Tis marvelous,
Prodigious,
Room, room,
She passes
Through the air
Like lightning.

THE VOICE OF HOFFMAN (outside).

Olympia!

SPALANZANI.

Stop them!

THE CHORUS.

Who of us will do it?

NICKLAUSSE.

She will break his head.

(Hoffman and Olympia re-appear. Nicklausse rushes to stop them.)

A thousand devils!

(He is violently struck and falls in an arm chair.)

THE CHORUS.

Patatra!...

SPALANZANI (jumping in).

Halt!

(He touches Olympia on the shoulder. She stops suddenly. Hoffman, exhausted, falls on a sofa).

There!

(To Olympia) Enough, enough, my child.

OLYMPIA.

Yes.

SPALANZANI.

No more waltzing.

OLYMPIA.

Yes.

SPALANZANI (to Cochenille).

You, Cochenille,
Take her back.

(He touches Olympia.)

COCHENILLE (pushing Olympia).

Go on, Go!

OLYMPIA.

Yes.

(Going out, slowly, pushed by Cochenille.)

Ha, ha, ha, ha, ha, ha, ha!

THE CHORUS.

What can we possibly say?
'Tis an exquisite girl,
She wants in nothing,
She does very well!

NICKLAUSSE (dolorous voice, pointing to Hoffman).

Is he dead?

SPALANZANI (examining Hoffman).

No! in fact
His eye glass is broken.
He is reviving.

THE CHORUS.

Poor young man!

COCHENILLE (outside).

Ah!

(He enters, very agitated.)

SPALANZANI.

What?

COCHENILLE.

The man with the glasses... there!

SPALANZANI.

Mercy! Olympia!...

HOFFMAN.

Olympia!...

(Sound of breaking springs with much noise).

SPALANZANI.

Ah, heaven and earth, she is broken!

HOFFMAN.

Broken!

COPPÉLIUS (entering).

Ha, ha, ha, ha, yes. Smashed!

(Hoffman rushes out. Spalanzani and Coppélius go at each other, fighting.)

SPALANZANI.

Rascal!

COPPÉLIUS.

Robber!

SPALANZANI.

Brigand!

COPPÉLIUS.

Pagan!

SPALANZANI.

Bandit!

COPPÉLIUS.

Pirate!

HOFFMAN (pale and terror stricken).

An automaton, an automaton.

(He falls into an armchair. General laughter.)

THE CHORUS.

Ha, ha, ha, the bomb has burst,
He loved an automaton.

SPALANZANI (despairingly).

My automaton.

ALL.

An automaton,
Ha, ha, ha, ha!

ACT III.

(In Venice. A gallery, in festival attire, in a palace on the Grand Canal.)

(The guests of GIULIETTA are grouped about on cushions.)

Barcarole.

GIULIETTA AND NICKLAUSSE (in the wings).

Oh soft night, oh night of love,
Smile on our bliss serene,
All the stars that shine above
Surround the heaven's queen!
Time it flies without return,
Forgetting our tenderness!
Far from thee I'll ever burn,
In lonely strait and stress.
Passioned zephyrs
Waft your caresses,
Passioned zephyrs
Soft are your kisses.
O soft night, oh night of love,
Smile on our bliss serene;
All the stars that shine above
Surround the heaven's queen.

(Giulietta and Nicklausse enter.)

HOFFMAN.

For me, by Jove, that is not what's enchanting!
At the feet of the beauty who gives us joy
Does pleasure sigh?
No, with laughing mouth no sorrows 'ere descanting.

BACCHIC SONG.

Friends... love tender with terror,
    Error!
Love in noise and wine!
    Divine
That a burning desire
Your heart enflames
In the fevers of pleasure
Consume your soul!
Transports of love,
Last a day
To the devil he who weeps
For two soft eyes,
To us the better bliss
Of joyous cries!
Let's live a day
In heaven.

THE CHORUS.

To the devil whoever weeps
For two soft eyes!
To us the better bliss
Of joyous song
We'll live a day
In Heaven!

HOFFMAN.

The sky lends you its brightness,
    Beauty,
But you hide in hearts of steel,
    Hell!
Bliss of paradise
Where love meets,
Oaths, cursed spirits,
    Dreams of life!
    Oh chastity,
    Oh purity,
    Lies!

THE CHORUS.

To the devil those who weep,
    etc., etc.

SCHLEMIL (entering).

  I see all is joy. Congratulations, madame.

GUILIETTA.

  What! Why, I've wept for you three whole days.

PITICHINACCIO.

  Good.

SCHLEMIL (to Pitichinaccio).

  Microbe!

PITICHINACCIO.

  Hola!

GIULIETTA.

Calm yourselves!
We have a strange poet among us.

(Presenting) Hoffman!

SCHLEMIL (with bad grace).

  Monsieur!

HOFFMAN.

Monsieur!

GIULIETTA (to Schlemil).

Smile on us, I beg,
And come take your place
At pharaoh!

THE CHORUS.

Bravo! To pharaoh!

(Giulietta after having invited all to follow her, goes toward door.
Hoffman offers his hand to Giulietta. Schlemil comes between.)

SCHLEMIL (taking Giulietta's hand).

By heavens!

GIULETTA.

To the game, gentlemen, to the game!

THE CHORUS.

To the game, the game!

(All go out except Hoffman and Nicklausse.)

NICKLAUSSE.

One word! I have two horses saddled. At the first dream
That Hoffman permits himself, I carry him off.

HOFFMAN.

And what dream ever could be born
By such realities?
Does one love a courtezan?

NICKLAUSSE.

 Yet this Schlemil...

HOFFMAN.
 I am not Schlemil.

NICKLAUSSE.

 Take care, the devil is clever.

DAPERTUTTO (appears at back).

HOFFMAN.

Were it so,
If he makes me love her, may he damn me,
Come!

NICKLAUSSE.

 Let us go.

(They go out.)

DAPERTUTTO (alone).

Yes!... to fight you.
The eyes of Giulietta are a sure weapon,
It needed that Schlemil fail,
Faith of captain and soldier,

You'll do like him.
I will that Giulietta shall use sorcery on you.

(Drawing from his finger a ring with a big sparkling diamond.)

Turn, turn, mirror, where the lark is caught,
Sparkle diamond, fascinate, draw her...
  The lark or the woman
  To this conquering bait
  Comes with wing or with heart;
One leaves her life, the other her soul.
Turn, turn, mirror where the lark is caught.
Sparkle, diamond, fascinate, attract her.

(Giulietta appears and advances fascinated toward the diamond that
Dapertutto holds towards her.)

DAPERTUTTO (placing the ring on Giuliettas finger).

GIULIETTA.

  What do you await from your servant?

DAPERTUTTO.

Good, you have divined
At seducing hearts above all others wise,
You have given me
The shade of Schlemil! I vary
My pleasures and I pray you
To get for me to-day
The reflection of Hoffman!

GIULIETTA.

  What! his reflection.

DAPERTUTTO.

Yes.
His reflection! You doubt
The power of your eyes?

GIULIETTA.

No.

DAPERTUTTO.

Who knows. Your Hoffman dreams, perhaps better.
(Severely) Yes, I was there, a while back, listening.
(With irony) He defies you...

GIULIETTA.

Hoffman? 'tis well!... From this day
I'll make him my plaything.

(Hoffman enters.)

DAPERTUTTO.

'Tis he!

(Dapertutto goes out. Hoffman intends to do the same.)

GIULIETTA (to Hoffman).

You leave me.

HOFFMAN (mockingly).

I have lost everything.

GIULIETTA.

What? you too...
Ah, you do me wrong.
Without pity, without mercy,
Go!... Go!...

HOFFMAN.

Your tears betrayed you.
Ah! I love you... even at the price of my life.

GIULIETTA.

Ah, unfortunate, but you do not know
That an hour, a moment, may prove fatal?
That my love will cost your life if you remain?
That Schlemil, this night, may strike you in my arms?
  Listen to my prayer;
  My life is wholly yours.
Everywhere I promise to accompany your steps.

HOFFMAN.

Ye gods with what bliss ye fire my heart?
Like a concert divine your voice does move me;
With a fire soft yet burning my being is devoured;
Your glances in mine have spent their flame,
Like radiant stars
And I feel, my well beloved,
Pass your perfumed breath
On my lips and on my eyes.

GIULIETTA.

Yet, to-day, strengthen my courage
By leaving me something of you!

HOFFMAN.

What do you mean?

GIULIETTA.
Listen and don't laugh at me.

(She takes Hoffman in her arms and finds a mirror.)

What I want is your faithful image,
To reproduce your features, your look, your visage,
The reflection that I see above me bend.

HOFFMAN.
My reflection? What folly!

GIULIETTA.

No! for it can detach itself
From the polished glass
And come quite whole in my heart to hide.

HOFFMAN.

In your heart?

GIULIETTA.

In my heart. 'Tis I who beg thee,
Hoffman, give me my wish.

HOFFMAN.

My reflection?

GIULIETTA.

Your reflection. Yes, wisdom or folly,
I await, I demand.

(Ensemble.)

HOFFMAN.

Ecstasy, unappeased bliss,
Strange and soft terror,
My reflection, my soul, my life
To you, always to you!

GIULIETTA.

If your presence I lose,
I would keep of you
Your reflection, your soul, your life;
Dear one, give them me.

GIULIETTA (suddenly).

  Schlemil!

(Schlemil enters followed by Nicklausse, Dapertutto, Pittichinaccio
and others.)

SCHLEMIL.

I was sure of it! Together!
Come, gentlemen, come,
'Tis for Hoffman, it seems to me
That we are abandoned.

(Ironic laughter.)

HOFFMAN.

Monsieur!

GIULIETTA (to Hoffman).

Silence!

(Aside) I love you, he has my key.

PITICHINACCIO (to Schlemil).

Let us kill him.

SCHLEMIL.

Patience!

DAPERTUTTO (to Hoffman).

How pale you are!

HOFFMAN.

Me!

DAPERTUTTO (showing him a mirror).

See rather.

HOFFMAN (amazed).

Heavens!

GIULIETTA.

Listen, gentlemen,
Here come the gondolas,
The hour of barcaroles
And of farewells!

(Schlemil conducts the guests out. Giulietta goes away throwing a look at Hoffman. Dapertutto remains. Nicklausse goes toward Hoffman.)

NICKLAUSSE.

Are you coming?

HOFFMAN.

Not yet.

NICKLAUSSE.

Why? Very well. I understand, Good-by.

(Aside). But I'll watch over him.

(He goes out.)

SCHLEMIL.

What do you wait for?

HOFFMAN.

That you give me a certain key I've sworn to have.

SCHLEMIL.

You shall have this key, sir, only with my life.

HOFFMAN.

Then I shall have one and the other.

SCHLEMIL.

That remains to be seen. On guard!

DAPERTUTTO.

You have no sword (presenting his own). Take mine!

HOFFMAN.

Thank you.

CHORUS (in the wings).

Sweet night, oh night of love,
Smile on our bliss serene
When the stars that shine above
Greet the heaven'ly Queen.

(Hoffman and Schlemil fight. Schlemil falls mortally wounded. Hoffman bends and takes the key from around his neck. He rushes to Giulietta's room. Giulietta appears in a gondola.)

HOFFMAN (coming back).

No one.

GIULIETTA (laughing).

Ha, ha, ha!

(Hoffmann is in a stupor looking at Giulietta.)

DAPERTUTTO (to Giulietta).

What will you do with him now?

GIULIETTA.

I'll turn him over to you.

PITICHINACCIO (entering the gondola)

Dear angel.

(Giulietta takes him in her arms.)

HOFFMAN (comprehending the infamy of Giulietta).

Vile wretch!

NICKLAUSSE.

Hoffman! Hoffman–the police!

(Nicklausse drags Hoffmann away. Giulietta and Pitichinaccia laugh.)

ACT IV.

(At Munich at CRESPEL'S. A room furnished in a bizarre fashion.)

ANTONIA (alone. She is seated at the clavichord).

She has fled, the dove
She has fled far from thee!

(She stops and rises.)

Ah memory too sweet, image too cruel!
Alas at my knees I hear, I see him!
She has fled, the dove.
She has fled far from thee;
She is faithful ever,
And she keeps her troth.
Beloved, my voice calls thee,
All my heart is thine.

(She approaches the clavichord again.)

Dear flower but now open,
In pity answer me,
Thou that knowest if still he loves me,
If he keeps his troth.
Beloved my voice implores thee.
May thy heart come to me.

(She falls in a chair.)

CRESPEL (entering suddenly).

Unhappy child, beloved daughter,
You promised to no longer sing.

ANTONIA.

My mother in me lived again;
My heart while singing thought it heard her.

CRESPEL.

There is my torment. Thy loved mother
Left thee her voice. Vain regrets!
Through thee I hear her. No, no, I beg...

ANTONIA (sadly).

Your Antonia will sing no more!

(She goes out slowly.)

CRESPEL (alone).

Despair! A little while again
I saw those spots of fire
Mark her face. God!
Must I lose her I adore?
Ah, that Hoffman... 'tis he
Who put in her heart this craze. I fled
Far as Munich...

(Enter Frantz.)

CRESPEL.

You, Frantz, open to nobody.

FRANTZ (false exit).

You think so...

CRESPEL.

Where are you going?

FRANTZ.

I'm going to see if anybody rang.
As you said...

CRESPEL.

I said, Open to nobody.
(Shouting) To nobody! This time do you hear?

FRANTZ.

 Good Heavens! we're not all of us deaf?

CRESPEL.

 All right! The devil take you!

FRANTZ.

 Yes, sir, the key is in the door.

CRESPEL.

 Idiot! donkey!

FRANTZ.

 Its agreed then.

CRESPEL.

 Morbleu!

(He exits quickly.)

FRANTZ (alone).

Well! What! angry always!
Strange, peevish, exacting!
One would think that one pleased him
For his money...
Day and night I'm on all fours,
At the least sign I'm silent;
It is just as if I sang!
But no, if I sang,
His contempt he'd have to modify.
I sing alone sometimes,
But singing isn't easy!
Tra la, la, tra, la la!
Still it isn't voice that I lack, I think,
Tra la la, tra la la,
No, 'tis the method.
Of course one can't have everything.
I sing pretty badly,
But dance agreeably,
And I do not flatter myself;
Dancing shows off my advantages.
'Tis my one great attraction,
But dancing isn't easy.
Tra la la, tra la la.

(He dances and stops.)

With women the shape of my leg
Would do me no harm,
Tra la la, tra la la!

(He falls.)

No, 'tis the method.

(Hoffman enters followed by Nicklausse.)

HOFFMAN.

Frantz! This is it. (touches Frantz on shoulder.)

Up, my friend.

FRANTZ.

Hey, who's there? (rises, surprised.)

Monsieur Hoffman!

HOFFMAN.

  Myself. Well, Antonia?

FRANTZ.

  He's gone out, sir.

HOFFMAN (laughing).

Ha, ha, deafer yet
Than last year...

FRANTZ.

Monsieur honors me,
I am very well, thanks to heaven.

HOFFMAN.

  Antonia! I must see her.

FRANTZ.

Very well! what a joy
For monsieur Crespel! (He goes out.)

HOFFMAN (sitting before the clavichord).

'Tis a song of love
That flies away,
Sad or gay;
It takes its turn...

ANTONIA (entering suddenly).

Hoffman!...

HOFFMAN (receiving her in his arms).

Antonia!

NICKLAUSSE (aside).

I am one too many, good night.

(He exits.)

ANTONIA.

Ah, I well knew that you loved me still.

HOFFMAN.

My heart told me that I was regretted,
But why were we separated?

ANTONIA.

I do not know.

(Ensemble.)

HOFFMAN.

I have happiness in my heart;
To-morrow you'll be my wife
    Happy couple.
The future shall be ours!
To love let's be faithful,
That her eternal chains,
    Keep our hearts
Conquerors even against time!

ANTONIA.

I have joy in my heart!
To-morrow I'll be your wife,
    Happy couple,
The future is ours!
Each day new songs,
Your genius opens its wings,
My conquering song
Is the echo of your heart.

HOFFMAN (smiling).

Still, oh my affianced,
Shall I speak my thought?
That, spite of myself, troubles me,
Music inspires a little jealousy,
You love it too much!

ANTONIA (smiling).

See the strange fantasy!
Did I love you for it, or it for you?
For you are not going to forbid me
To sing, as did my father.

HOFFMAN.

What say you?

ANTONIA.

Yes, my father at present imposes the virtue
Of silence.

HOFFMAN (aside).

'Tis strange... can it be?...

ANTONIA (drawing him to the clavichord).

Come here as before;
Listen, and you'll see if I've lost my voice.

HOFFMAN.

How your eye lights up, your hand trembles.

ANTONIA (making him sit down).

Here, the soft song of love we sang together.

(She sings.)

'Tis a song of love
That flies off
Sad or joyful,
Turn by turn,
'Tis a song of love,
The new rose
Smiles on the Spring.
Ah! how long will it be
That it lives?

TOGETHER.

'Tis a song of love
That flies off, etc., etc.

HOFFMAN.

A ray of flame
Matches thy beauty.
Will you see the summer?
Flower of the soul.

TOGETHER.

'Tis a song of love, etc., etc.

(Antonia puts her hand to her heart.)

HOFFMAN.

Why, what is the matter?

ANTONIA (doing same again).

Nothing.

HOFFMAN (listening).

Chut.

ANTONIA.

Heavens, my father! Come, come...

(She goes out.)

HOFFMAN.

No! I must know the last word of this mystery.

(He hides. Crespel appears.)

CRESPEL (looking about him).

No, nothing. I thought Hoffman was here.
May he go to the devil!

HOFFMAN (aside).

Many thanks!

FRANTZ (entering).

Sir.

CRESPEL.

What?

FRANTZ.

Doctor Miracle.

CRESPEL.

Infamous scoundrel,
Quickly close the door.

FRANTZ.

Yes, sir, the doctor...

CRESPEL.

He, doctor? No, on my soul,
A grave digger, an assassin!
Who would kill my daughter after my wife.
I hear the jingle of his golden vials,
From me let him be chased.

(Miracle suddenly appears. Frantz runs away.)

MIRACLE.

 Ha, ha, ha, ha!

CRESPEL.

Well, here I am! 'tis me.
This good monsieur Crespel, I like him,
But where is he?

CRESPEL (stopping him).

 Morbleu!

MIRACLE.

Ha, ha, ha, ha!
I sought for your Antonia.
Well, this trouble she inherited
From her mother? Still progressing, dear girl.
We'll cure her. Take me to her.

CRESPEL.

To assassinate her... If you make one step
I'll throw you out of the window.

MIRACLE.

There now softly, I do not wish to
Displease you.

(He advances a chair.)

CRESPEL.

  What do you, traitor?

MIRACLE.

To minimize the danger,
One must know it.
Let me question her.

CRESPEL AND HOFFMAN.

  Terror penetrates me.

(Ensemble.)

(Miracle, his hand extended toward Antonia's room.)

To my conquering power,
Give way with good grace.
Near me without terror
Come take your place.

CRESPEL AND HOFFMAN.

With fright and with horror
All my being is cold;
A strange terror
Chains me to this place.
  I'm afraid.

CRESPEL (seating himself).

Come, speak and be brief.

(Miracle continues his magnetic passes. The door of Antonia's room opens slowly. Miracle indicates that he takes Antonia's hand and leads her to a chair.)

MIRACLE.

Please sit there.

CRESPEL.

I am seated.

MIRACLE (paying no attention).

How old are you, please?

CRESPEL.

Who, me?

MIRACLE.

I am speaking to your child.

HOFFMAN (aside).

Antonia.

MIRACLE.

What age (he listens). Twenty!

CRESPEL.

What?

MIRACLE.

The Spring of life.

(He appears to feel the pulse.)

Let me see your hand!...

CRESPEL.

The hand.

MIRACLE (pulling out his watch).

Chut! let me count.

HOFFMAN (aside).

God! am I the plaything of a dream? Is it a ghost?

MIRACLE.

The pulse is unequal and fast, bad symptom. Sing.

CRESPEL (rising).

No, no, don't speak... don't have her sing.

(The voice of Antonia is heard.)

MIRACLE.

See her face brightens, her eyes are on fire;
She carries her hand to her beating heart.

(He follows Antonia with his gestures. The door of her room closes quickly.)

CRESPEL.

  What is he saying?

MIRACLE (rising).

It would be a pity truly
To leave to death so fine a prey!

CRESPEL.

  Shut up!

MIRACLE.

If you will accept my help,
If you would save her days,
I have there certain vials I keep in reserve.

(He takes vials from pocket which he makes sound like castanets.)

CRESPEL.

  Shut up!

MIRACLE.

  Of which you should.

CRESPEL.

Shut up! Heaven preserve me
From listening to your advice, miserable assassin.

MIRACLE.

 Of which you should, each morning...

(Ensemble.)

MIRACLE.

Why, yes, I hear you.
A while ago, an instant
These vials, poor father,
You will be then, I hope,
   Satisfied.

CRESPEL.

Be off, be off, be off!
Out of this house, Satan,
Beware of the anger
And the sorrow of a father.
   Be off!

HOFFMAN (aside).

From the death that awaits thee
I shall know, poor child,
How tear thee away, I hope!
Laugh in vain at a father,
   Satan!

MIRACLE (continuing with same coolness).

 Of which you should...

CRESPEL.

Be off!

MIRACLE.

Each morning...

CRESPEL.

Be off!

(He pushes Miracle out and closes the door.)

Ah, he's outside and my door is closed!
We are at last alone,
My beloved girl!

MIRACLE (walking through the wall).

Of which you should each morning...

CRESPEL.

Ah, wretch,
Come, come, may the waves engulf thee!
 We'll see if the devil
 Will get thee out.

CRESPEL.

Be off, be off, be off!
   etc., etc.

HOFFMAN (aside).

From the death that awaits thee,
   etc., etc.

MIRACLE.

Of which you should...

CRESPEL.

Get out!

MIRACLE.

Each morning...

CRESPEL.

Get out!

(They disappear together.)

HOFFMAN (coming down).

To sing no more! How obtain from her
Such a sacrifice?

ANTONIA (appearing).

Well? What did my father say?

HOFFMAN.

Ask me nothing;
Later you'll know all; a new road
Opens for us, my Antonia!...
To follow my steps dismiss from your memory
These dreams of future success and glory
That your heart to mine confided.

ANTONIA.

 But yourself!

HOFFMAN.

Love calls to both of us,
All that is not you is nothing in my life.

ANTONIA.

 Very well! Here is my hand!

HOFFMAN.

Ah dear Antonia, shall I appreciate
What you do for me? (He kisses her hands.)

Your father will perhaps return.
I leave you... until to-morrow.

ANTONIA.

 Until to-morrow.

(Hoffman goes out.)

ANTONIA (opening one of the doors).

Of my father easily he has become the accomplice,
But come, regrets are superfluous,
I promised him. I shall sing no more.

(She falls in a chair.)

The Tales of Hoffmann

MIRACLE (appearing suddenly behind her.)

You will sing no more. Do you know what a sacrifice?
He imposes on your youth, and have you measured it?
Grace, beauty, talent, sacred gift;
All these blessings that heaven gave for your share,
Must they be hid in the shadow of a household?
Have you not heard, in a proud dream,
Like unto a forest by the wind moving,
Like a soft shiver of the pressing crowd
That murmurs your name and follows you with its eyes?
There is the ardent joy and the eternal festival,
That the flower of your years is about to abandon,
For the middle class pleasures where they would enchain you,
And the squalling children who will give you less beauty!

ANTONIA (without turning round).

Ah, what is this voice that troubles my spirit?
Is it Hell that speaks or Heaven that warns me?
No! happiness is not there, oh cursed voice,
And against my pride my love has armed me;
Glory is not worth the happy shade whence invites me
The house of my beloved.

MIRACLE.

What loves can now be yours,
Hoffman sacrifices you to his brutality,
He only loves in you your beauty,
And for him as for the others.
Soon will come the time of infidelity.

(He disappears.)

ANTONIA (rising).

No, do not tempt me! go away,
Demon! I will no longer listen.
I have sworn to be his, my beloved awaits me,

I'm no longer my own and I can't take myself back;
And a few moments since, on his heart adored
What eternal love did he not pledge me;
Who will save me from the demon, from myself?
My mother, my mother, I love her.

(She falls weeping on the clavichord.)

MIRACLE (re-appears behind Antonia)

Your mother? Dare you invoke her?
Your mother? But is it not she?
Who speaks by my voice ingrate, and recalls to you
The splendor of the name that you would abdicate?

(The portrait lights up and becomes animated.)

  Listen!

THE VOICE.

  Antonia!

ANTONIA.

Heavens!... my mother, my mother!

THE GHOST.

Dear child whom I call,
As I used to do,
'Tis your mother, 'tis she,
Listen to her voice.

ANTONIA.

  Mother!

MIRACLE.

Yes, yes, 'tis her voice, do you hear?
Her voice, best counselor,
Who leaves you a talent the world has lost!

THE GHOST.

Antonia!

MIRACLE.

Listen! She seems to live aagin,
And the distant public by its bravos fills her bliss.

ANTONIA.

Mother!

GHOST.

Antonia!

MIRACLE.

Join with her.

ANTONIA.

Yes, her soul calls me
As before;
'Tis my mother, 'tis she
I hear her voice.

THE GHOST.

Dear child whom I call
As I used to do;
'Tis your mother, 'tis she;
List to her voice.

ANTONIA.

No, enough, I cannot!

MIRACLE.

Again.

ANTONIA.

I will sing no more.

MIRACLE.

Again.

ANTONIA.

What ardor draws and devours me?

MIRACLE.

Again! Why stop?

ANTONIA (out of breath).

I give way to a transport that maddens,
What flame is it dazzles my eyes
A single moment to live,

And my soul flies to Heaven.

THE GHOST.

Dear child whom I call,
    etc., etc.

ANTONIA.

'Tis my mother, 'tis she,
    etc., etc.

ANTONIA.

Ah!

(She falls dying on the sofa. Miracle sinks in the earth uttering a peal of laughter.)

CRESPEL (running in).

My child... my daughter... Antonia!.

ANTONIA (expiring).

My father! Listen, 'tis my mother
Who calls me. And he... has returned...
'Tis a song of love,
Flies away,
Sad or joyful...

(She dies.)

CRESPEL.

No... a single word... just one... my child... speak!
Come, speak! Execrable death!

No! pity, mercy... go away!

HOFFMAN (coming hurriedly).

Why these cries?

CRESPEL.

Hoffman!... ah wretch!
'Tis you who killed her!...

HOFFMAN (rushing to Antonia).

Antonia!

CRESPEL (beside himself).

Blood to color her cheek. A weapon.
A knife!...

(He seizes a knife and attacks Hoffman.)

NICKLAUSSE (entering and stopping Crespel).

Unhappy man!

HOFFMAN (to Nicklausse).

Quick! give the alarm;
A doctor... a doctor!...

MIRACLE (appearing).

Present!

(He feels Antonia's pulse.)

Dead!

CRESPEL (crazy).

Ah, God, my child, my daughter!

HOFFMAN (despairingly).

Antonia!

EPILOGUE.

(Same scene as First Act. The various personages are in the same positions they were in at the end of First Act.)

HOFFMANN.

There is the story
Of my loves,
And the memory
In my heart will always remain.

CHORUS.

Bravo, bravo, Hoffmann.

HOFFMANN.

Ah, I am mad. For us the craze divine,
The spirits of alcohol, of beer and of wine,
For us intoxication,
Chaos where we forget.

NICKLAUSSE.

Ah, I understand, three dramas in a drama, Olympia...

HOFFMANN.

Smashed!

NICKLAUSSE.

Antonia...

HOFFMANN.

Dead!

NICKLAUSSE.

Giulietta...

HOFFMANN.

Oh, for her, the last verse of the song of Klein-Zach.
When he drank too much gin or rack,
You ought to have seen the two tails at his back,
Like lilies in a lac,
The monster made a sound of flick flack,
   Flic, flac,
   There's Klein-Zach.

CHORUS.

   Flick flack,
   There's Klein-Zach.

CHORUS.

Light up the punch, drunk we'll get;
And may the weakest
Roll under the table;
Luther was a goodly man,
Tire lan laire, tire lan la,
   etc., etc.

(The students tumultuously go in the next room. Hoffmann remains
as if in a stupor.)

THE MUSE (appearing in an aureole of light).

And I? I, the faithful friend,
Whose hand wiped thy tears?
By whom thy latent sorrow
Exhales in heavenly dreams?
Am I nothing? May the tempest
Of passion pass away in thee!
The man is no more; the poet revives
I love thee Hoffmann! be mine!
Let the ashes of thy heart fire thy genius,
Whose serenity smiles on thy sorrows.
The Muse will soften thy blessed sufferings.
One is great by love but greater by tears.

(She disappears.)

HOFFMANN (alone).

Oh God! what ecstasy embraces my soul,
Like a concert divine Thy voice hath moved me,
With soft and burning fire my being is devoured,
Thy glances in mine have suffused their flame,
Like radiant stars.
And I feel, beloved Muse,
Thy perfumed breath flutter
On my lips and on my eyes!

(He falls face on table.)

STELLA (approaching slowly).

  Hoffmann? asleep...

NICKLAUSSE.

  No, dead drunk. Too late, madame.

LINDORF.

Corbleu!

NICKLAUSSE.

Oh, here is the counselor, Lindorf, who awaits you.

(Stella keeps her eyes on Hoffmann and throws a flower at his feet as she goes out with Lindorf.)

THE END.

BARCAROLE - INTERMEZZO

from "The Tales of Hoffman," by JACQUES OFFENBACH.

Engraved by LilyPond (version 2.4.2)

CPSIA information can be obtained
at www.ICGtesting.com
Printed in the USA
BVHW072109040121
596832BV00006B/646